# Find Work Through

# Temporary Agencies

## A Survival Guide to the New Economy
## Copyright 2009 By Daniel G. Jennings

## 1. Why Everybody Needs to Use Temporary Agencies

Job hunting is hard even in the best of times and almost impossible in a tough economy like we're facing right now. Most of us hate searching for employment and rightly so job hunting is hard work. The endless hours of searching, networking, attending job fairs, sending out resumes, visiting employment agencies and making phone calls. Searching for a job is often harder work than the tasks we will perform on the job itself.

Now what if I told you that there was a cadre of hard working professionals who were willing to go out and search for employment you. Professionals who have far more contacts, resources and experience searching for work than you do. Best of all these professionals won't charge you a cent, you pay nothing for their services and they will find you a job.

Does it sound too good to be true? Well it is not, those professionals are out there right now in your community they work at businesses called temporary agencies.

Temporary agencies make their money by providing employees to businesses, government and other organizations. The temporary agency acts as the employer, they hire the employee, handle the background checks and other human resources chores and pay the salary and benefits. The employer pays the employee's salary or wage to the temporary agency and the agency takes a cut of the pay to make its money.

The main reason employers use temporary agencies is to save money. Hiring a person is very expensive these days, an employer has to do a background check, drug tests, skills testing and a job search to find an employee. Many employers don't have these resources so they turn to temporary agencies. They effectively outsource their human resources department by hiring temporary agencies.

Other organizations turn to temp agencies because they only need employees on a short term or seasonal basis. Say a factory that needs some help just to fill a special order or a store that's gearing up for the holiday rush. Many employers use temporaries to take the places of workers who are on leave or vacation. Its also common for organizations that don't have a local HR office to use temporary agencies.

Everybody should know about temporary agencies and take advantage of the services they offer because the line between temporary and permanent work is blurring. Many big corporations and other employers use temporary agencies to fill positions that is they bring in a temp to fill a position and if the temp works out they offer her a full time job. Businesses that aren' t sure that they will have the resources to offer permanent employees may use temporaries as a high percentage of their workforce.

There are also many cases in which a company only needs help for a few days or weeks. It makes no sense to hire a full time worker and let him go after a few days if there isn' t enough work. A temp can be brought into cover only that work saving the company the expense of hiring a full time worker.

The main reason you should be using temporary agencies in your job search is because temp work can lead to a full time job. Temporary work is often a try out for a full time job, the employer gets to know you and see if you can do the work and fit in at their workplace. A temp who does a really good job and impresses the bosses can be offered a permanent position.

This happened to me; I took a temporary job as a scanner and accounts payable clerk at TeleTech Holdings Inc in Englewood, Colorado in April, 2006. I worked hard at this job for five months and impressed my boss. In September, 2006, I was offered full time permanent employment with a good salary and full benefits at TeleTech as Accounts Payable Coordinator. I held that position for over two years until December, 2008.

Temporary work can lead to a full time job and it can be fun.

There are other benefits to temporary work as well I would have never gotten into accounts payable work in which I have found three well paying jobs if it hadn't been for temporary work. I became available of the opportunities in AP because I took a temporary position in AP through Kelly Services. Temporary work is a great way to learn about the job market and the opportunities in your community.

As a temporary worker I learned a wide variety of skills that I could not have gotten elsewhere. For example I learned how to use scanners and high volume copiers, two skills that have helped me land a number of jobs. I also gained valuable knowledge of printing and shipping and receiving through temporary work. Temporary work also exposed me to a variety of job environments including office work.

Temporary work is a great way to get experience and skills that you can put on your resume. For recent college graduates or students temporary work can give you at least some experience. You can at least say you did some work in the field that you're applying int.

Another advantage to temporary work is that it gives you first hand experience working in a business or industry. You can actually see what the work is like and if you' d like doing it on a long term basis. If you' re thinking of switching careers or industries, doing some temporary work in the fields you' re interested in can show you if you would actually enjoy working in that field. It can also prepare you for the conditions to expect when you start looking for a permanent position.

Temporary work is also fun you get to visit a wide variety of work places and experience different jobs. You get to meet lots of new people, make new friends and find new contacts that can help you in career and job search. You get new skills you can put on your resume and people you can use as references.

A temporary job also gives you a paycheck in exchange for doing all of these things. You get paid to go out and sample the job market and make new contacts. Even if you just pick up a few extra bucks that' s money that you can use. If you' re laid off or seeking a job, temporary work can help you pay bills or give you the money to have a little fun. Temporary jobs are a great source of income at a time when a lot of us simply can' t rely on traditional employment.

The best part of temporary employment is that when you sign on with a temporary agency you get a professional recruiter out there working for you. The recruiters at temporary agencies make their money by placing people in jobs so they have an incentive to find work for you.

The temporary agency employees also have resources and contacts that you don't. Temp recruiters know who's actually hiring in your community and who isn't. They also have direct contacts with HR people and executives at companies that you don't. They know who to call and who to send a resume to, to get someone hired. Temp agency workers spend a lot of time cultivating contacts at employers and networking. They often know of jobs in your community that aren't being advertised and opportunities you won't hear of on the grapevine.

Developing a good relationship with the people at temporary agencies in your area will allow you to network with lots of employers you'd never get close to. Your resume will be put in front of many executives who would not normally see it and more importantly there will be someone there selling you to the employer.

Temporary agency recruiters are salespeople their job is to sell you to employers. When you register with a temporary agency you just engaged a sales professional to go out and sell you to employers.

This means that everybody who is looking for work, thinking of switching jobs or facing a layoff should register with as many temporary agencies as possible. Temporary agencies are the greatest bargain in job hunting. All you have to invest is a little of your time and perhaps a bit of gas driving to interview at the temp agency and you can get the services of a professional job hunter at your disposal.

Nor are temporary agencies restricted to any particular kind of business originally temporary agencies provided mostly female clerical work. Today they employ people in all fields and jobs laborers, engineers, IT professionals, janitors, even management. All manner of employers use temporary agencies including state, local and federal government. Some school districts use temporary agencies to fill substitute teacher jobs. No matter what field you are in there are probably temporary jobs available in that field. Even many working class jobs like truck driver and fork lift operator are now filled by temporary agencies.

Everybody needs to get registered with temporary agencies and stay registered if they want to work.

## 2.   What is a Temporary Agency?

Simply put a temporary agency is a firm that hires employees on a contract basis then charges a client for privilege of using those employees' services. When you work for a temporary agency, the agency is legally your employer but you perform the work for the client. As a temp you usually report to two bosses your supervisor who actually oversees you and your work and someone at the temporary agency who handles things like hiring, firing, pay, and other human resources chores.

There are many reasons why organizations uses temps, temps are cheaper than full time workers. They offer the flexibility to get a task accomplished without adding staff. Many organizations use temps because they are bound by state law or union contracts to give regular workers a set wage and benefits. Since temps are working are working for another firm they aren' t covered by those obligations.

Now a temporary agency is not a placement service, search firm or  a headhunter those business exist to find work for fulltime employees. Many big corporations use search firms when seeking to fill specialized or executive positions. A lot of high-level executives and the like use search firms when they' re looking for work. To make things confusing many temporary agencies do offer these services.

This is a big advantage to you because a temporary agency may also be trying to fill a full time job in your field. Always tell a temporary agency that you' ll be willing to take full time work because they maybe aware of a full time position for you. Many temporary agencies also automatically submit qualified resumes to positions their employees see advertised so your resume could reach a lot of people you didn' t intend to see it if you use a temp agency.

Nor are temporary agencies consulting firms, even though some temp agencies offer consulting services. Consulting services offer a company specialized expertise or advice in much the same way lawyers or engineers do except its usually business or technology related. A company may hire an accounting consulting firm to examine its accounts payable practices to see if they can be improved or modernized for example. Consulting firms offer companies expertise without the permanent commitment of hiring a full time employee.

Many people get temporary agencies and consulting firms confused because consultants sometimes work in the office much as temps do. In some cases consultants may actually be brought in to perform a specific task much as temps are. Don' t be adverse to consulting work it can pay well and its much like temp work. If you' re an older worker if a lot of expertise look into consulting work. Many companies use consulting agencies to get advice from experienced older workers.

A temporary agency functions like a company' s human resources department it takes resumes and applications evaluates them and decides whom to call in for an interview. After the interview it determines which person to offer a job to or which person' s resume it' ll send out to a client. If a person is hired the temporary agency will take care of the hiring chores such as the background and drug check. Once the person is on the job the temporary agency will pay his or her salary and benefits. If the person is laid off or fired the temporary agency will take of that chore to.

The great thing about a temporary agency from your standpoint is that when you go there, you' re applying to an HR department that represents several different, perhaps several dozen employers at once. Employers use temporary agencies to save time and money and so can you.

There are three kinds of temporary agencies operating in most communities: big national corporations, franchises and local independent agencies. You' re probably familiar with the big national temporary agencies: Manpower, Kelly Services, Adecco, Accountemps, Robert Half, Randstaad, Appleone, Etc. These are big multinational corporations with offices all over the place. They are all over the country and they may have several offices in a city. The great thing about these agencies is that you only have to sign up once and you' ll be registered with that company all over the world. (See Chapter 4 more details.)

Always register with all of the major national temporary agencies that operate in your area. That way you will be able to quickly apply for any job that they have available and you' ll be able to take advantage of their extensive network of contacts. Another advantage to going with the nationals is that many employers have exclusive contracts with one or two temporary agencies. Going through those agencies maybe the only way to get in the door at some employers.

A second kind of temporary agency is a franchise, the difference between a franchised agency and a corporate agency is that the corporate agencies are operated by employees of the corporation. The franchise is owned by a local individual who operates it, this person is called the franchisee. The company gives the franchise the rights to use their name and participate in their advertising and use corporate resources in exchange for a cut of the profits. Two examples of big franchised temp operations are Appleone and Express.

A local independent agency is a small business owned and operated by a person in your community. Most local agencies are small they usually employ only a couple of people and run by a temporary business professional often a veteran of a big national agency. Most local independent agencies specialize in placing people in one particular business such as accounting or retail. Local independent agencies can be good or bad depending on who ' s operating them.

A very similar business to temporary agencies that you may see operating in your community is a labor service. A labor service provides the most basic kind of worker a laborer with a pair of hands and a strong back. They fill the most menial jobs such as sweeping floors or moving boxes in a warehouse. Labor services do provide an important role they connect low level workers people who are often ignorant and illiterate with employers.

The major difference between labor services and temporary agencies is that labor services provide work on a day to day basis − hence the term day laborer. They often pay in cash or an easily cashed check. Many labor services even provide vehicles to haul workers to job sites because quite a few of their workers may not even have cars.

Most people should probably avoid labor services because they don' t pay well and the work they provide is boring and back breaking. However if you' re really strapped for cash or you know somebody who' s unqualified for regular work a labor service might be an alternative to consider. Some temporary agencies such as Manpower do operate labor services and most temporary agencies do fill laborer jobs. It should be noted that most laborers employed by temporary agencies are treated as normal temps.

Temporary agencies do fill a lot of the higher end labor jobs such as forklift and machine operators or shipping clerks, positions the require some education. So don' t overlook a temporary agency if you' re looking for a job in manufacturing or a warehouse.

### 3.  How to Find Temporary Agencies

Temporary agencies are real easy to find because they are businesses that make their money by locating people and putting them to work. Temporary agencies want you to find them and come in and apply for work.

The best place to look for  temporary agencies is on the Internet, simply do a web search for temporary agencies that operate in your area. Or write down the names of some of the big national agencies like Randstad, Kelly, Addecco, Manpower, Robert Half and its various subsidiaries and type them into search engine. Once you locate their websites you should be able to use the search features on the website to locate an office in your area.

Another great way to find temporary agencies is to check the big Internet job boards. Many temporary agencies advertise on Monster.com and Careerbuilder.com. Take a look at these sites and see what temporary agencies are advertising in your area. A look at these sites will also show you what jobs are available in your area and who's hiring. Some temporary agencies will also advertise through Craigslist but be warned some temporary agencies masquerade as employers seeking direct hire workers and post ads on Craigslist.

Another way to find temporary agencies in your area is to simply look around when you're driving, walking or riding a bicycle or motorcycle through the community. Some temporary agencies especially those that specialize in labor or more basic jobs will maintain store fronts or other offices. If you see a temporary agency you're unfamiliar with operating in your locale it might be a good idea to go in and check them out. Be warned these maybe labor services or fee chargers (see below).

When searching for temporary don' t neglect word of mouth ask people you know what temporary agencies they' re aware of and if they have contacts at those temporary agencies. In particular ask people you know who work at larger employers in your area such as government agencies or big corporations what temporary agencies their employers use. That way you can learn which temporary agencies actually place people and which don' t. At the same time you should also ask for contacts at the temporary agencies. If you are working even part time ask people working at your jobsite if they are temporaries and try to learn what temp agencies they use. Temporary agencies are always looking for good employees and sometimes pay bonuses for referrals of good employees. This means that those people should be happy to refer to you to their agency.

You can also make contact with temporary agencies through job fairs. Some temporary agencies put out booths at job fairs especially those sponsored by colleges and the ones you see advertised in the newspaper. Generally, I' d recommend avoiding job fairs unless they are sponsored by a college or are industry specific. The job fairs sponsored by local newspapers don' t provide many networking opportunities and the temp agencies there can probably be contacted quicker through your online efforts.

One final thought, the temporary agency market is always changing. New agencies are always opening and old ones are always closing so keep a close watch on it. Always be on the look out for new temporary agencies and try to get your resume to them as soon as you can.

### 4.   Registration

Once you' ve located the temporary agencies you want to use, comes the most important part registration. Registration simply means filling out the employment application and legal forms related to working for that company. It' s usually fast and quite easy. Some temporary agencies will ask you to come in and fill out forms by hand in their office but most especially the big national firms let you register online.

If you can register online for several reasons first because it is easier and quicker. If you' re like me you can probably type a lot faster than you can write and your typing is probably easier to read than your handwriting. Filling out a form in the leisure of your home rather than a temporary agency' s lobby means that you can take your time. You also have access to information like addresses and names of former employers or references at home you might not bring with you. You might even be able to cut and paste information from files on your computer into the agency's files. Many temporary agencies will even let you sign your registration on line through an electronic signature.

Some people will worry about security, most temporary agency websites are secure and the information they're asking you for is public record. Don't worry too much the only really important piece of information they're asking for is your social security number. If a temporary agency asks for your banking information you can provide it in paper at the office if you want. You can also print out the forms and take them to the temporary agency office with you, some agencies will ask for this.

Something to think about here is this, your information on file at the temporary agency is also vulnerable to identity theft. Somebody could break in and steal it or a dishonest employee there could simply copy it. There's also no guarantee that the temporary agency won't just toss its paper files into the trash without shredding them. There is no such thing as perfect security online or in the real world if you want to find employment you're going to have to give out data sooner or later.

The advantage to registering online is that you don' t have to go into the temporary agency unless they ask you for an interview. You can save yourself a lot of time and trouble by registering online.

Another advantage to registering online with large temporary agencies is that all of that temporary agency' s employees and offices can see it. That means that somebody at a distant office who' s trying to fill a job in your area can see your resume and place you on that job. This actually happened to me a temporary agency worker in Dallas saw my resume online and hired me for a couple of short term positions in Denver where I live.

When you do begin the registration process you should get ready first, have your resume available as a Microsoft Word Document. Most temporary agencies will ask you to upload it to their sites when you register. Then have the basic information they' re asking for available. This will include the names of your former employees, their addresses and phone numbers and the names addresses, phone numbers and e-mails of your former supervisors available. Also have your references available so you can quickly put them into the registration form. One time saving tip when registering online is to copy your information off of the document on your computer and paste it on to the site.

One suggestion here simply have a good basic version of your resume available the templates available in Microsoft Word are fine. Just create a resume that lists the basics, your job experience, your education etc. Anything else they ask for can be put on another sheet of paper. Keeping a resume simple makes it easy to read and remember a resume is a throwaway document. Most people who will see it will throw it away. Don' t bother putting salary, references or employer contact information on your resume most employers will ask you for that information anyway. Instead use your resume to advertise your skills, education, experience and accomplishments.

Sometimes temporary agencies will ask to revise your resume to suit their tastes. This doesn' t mean that there' s anything wrong with your resume they' re just showing off their smarts. One question I always have for such people but don' t ask is if my resume is so bad why did you look at it?

My suggestion would be to go along with them and make the revisions they want it won' t take long and it ' ll keep them happy. This will also establish you as cooperative which will mean they' ll be more likely to place you. Remember a resume is a throwaway document, that most people will glance at once so it pays to have a few different versions of it on your computer.

Many temporary agencies will also ask you for your job skills simply list every job skill have. Don' t just list the main ones, list them all if you normally do Accounts Payable work but have had Accounts Receivable experience in the past list that. It will make you more employable. List all of your rewards and accomplishments and any professional licenses or certification that you may have.

Sometimes the agency' s website will directly transfer information from your resume straight into the form. This can save time but it can also mess things up, whenever this happens go through all the data transferred from the resume to the form to make sure its correct and complete. Almost every time that I' ve done this the program transferring the data has messed something up. Pay particular attention to dates of employment these never come through properly.

If you have to go in and register at a temporary office make sure that you bring all of your information in. The best way to do this is to organize it into Word documents on your computer and print them out. This way the information will be at hand it' ll be easy to copy and easy to access and it' ll be organized. The information will also be available on a piece of paper you can hand to the temporary service employees or stick in your registration packet. Another advantage to this method is the fact that you ' ll be able to e-mail the documents to people who ask to see them.

Take your time filling out the registration and unless somebody at the temporary agency says otherwise you' ll have to fill it all out. This can be a time consuming chore but you may not be able to avoid it. Try and fill it out all out at the agency while you' re waiting. Asking to take the application home and bring it back makes you look unprofessional. Ask yourself this would you hire an adult who couldn' t sit down and fill out a few basic forms?

Remember if you fill out your application online always tell the people at the temporary agency. On numerous occasions I' ve had temp agencies employees ask me to fill out forms with information I' ve already entered online. Save yourself and them time and effort by telling them that you' ve registered online. Even if you' re registered online you might have to sign a form at the temporary agency.

If you do have to go in and register always bring two forms of identification such as your driver' s license and Social Security card or driver' s license and passport.

Federal law requires temporary agencies and all other employers to get two forms of ID to verify the fact that you are legally authorized to work in the company. Remember the IDs you bring in should be official IDs of some sort such as a driver' s license. Even if you don' t have a car you should get a driver' s license and keep it current for identification purposes.

Another tip have a scanner/fax machine available in your home in case a temporary service asks you to fax or e-mail them your documentation. I had a temporary agency in Dallas do this when I lived in Denver. You can now buy multiuse units that fax, copy and scan for less than $100 so anybody can do this. If you don' t have a landline for your fax you can use an online service like www.fax.com to send your fax. Services like this let you upload documents from your computer into their fax server which then sends them to the recipient. I use Fax.com which does a great job of sending Word Documents and PDFs as faxes. You can scan signed documents in and send them as a PDF if the recipient asks for a signed document.

Sometimes an out of town temporary agency will ask you to send them forms and other information. If they do, ask them to send you the information with a prepaid UPS, USPS or Fedex mailing label or have them send you such a label online. You should not be paying to mail them information that they' ve requested it is their responsibility to pay for it.

Related to registration is the testing this can either be done online or at the temporary agency. The tests they use are standardized and can be very confusing, but they use the same few tests. They' re pretty easy but clunky and hard to use. Some of them have been frustrating. In particular I' ve seen word and Excel tests that won' t let you put in the correct answer.

If you get a bad score on these tests ask the temporary agency if you can retake the test. Most will let you do it because the temporary agency is looking for is high scores on the tests. High scoring employees seem impressive and are more likely to get hired. Remember the temporary agency only gets paid if you get hired so they want you to look as good as possible to the potential employer.

How important these tests are is a matter of debate, some temporary agencies set great score by them and have told me that I haven' t got a job because of a low score. I ' ve also had temporary agency employees come out and tell me that these tests don' t matter.

It maybe possible to practice for the tests temporary agencies give particularly data entry tests. Many temp agencies want a high typing speed and KPM keystrokes per minute for data entry. The best way to get your speed up is to do a lot of practice, if you've had years of experience doing the job you should do fine but be careful. The conditions they test under aren't like working at the office. For example the programs they use won't let you go back and correct mistakes like you would if you were entering data. One helpful suggestion might be to find some practice programs online.

Sometimes a temporary agency will ask if you have reliable transportation. Just check yes on this box even if you don't have a car. Remember they're asking you if you reliable transportation. Its been my experience that public transportation, the bus, light rail and subways is far more reliable than some of the cars I've owned. If you use public transportation don't tell them unless they ask directly, sadly enough a lot of people believe that a person can't g et around the block if they don't have a car. Fortunately most temp agencies don't press the issue and don't care if you get to work on time everyday.

Register with as a many temporary agencies as you can there is no law or rule against registering with more than one temporary agency. You can register with as many temp agencies as you so do so. The temporary agencies themselves may not like it if you' re registered with more than one agency but believe me they like the fee they get from placing you more than they dislike your dalliance with their competitors. So register with as many temporary agencies as you can. Every time you register with a temporary agency you expand the network of professional recruiters that' s out there seeking work for you. When it comes to temporary agencies the more you' re registered with the better.

### 5. Interviewing at the Temp Agency

The most important aspect of your relationship with a temporary agency is your initial interview. If you go in and make a good impression and establish a really good relationship with the temporary agency you' ll have them on your side. They' ll like you and want to go out and find you work. They' ll feel confident sending you out to work with their clients and help you. They might even do you favors such as sending you out on interviews you might not normally get.

The reverse is also true if you make a really bad impression you' ll show the temporary agency that you will make a bad impression. They won' t want to send you out because they know you' re unprofessional or unreliable. They' ll just throw your resume away or quietly file it in some drawer where it will be quickly forgotten. You should remember that your initial interview maybe your only meeting with the temporary agency employees. The impressions you leave there could be all they know of you so if you leave a bad impression they' ll have a bad opinion of you and no incentive to try and find you work.

This means that you have to be on your toes when you interview at a temp agency. Always  treat a temporary agency like a job interview because that' s what it is. A job interview that can find you work with lots of different employers and open the door to a network of job contacts.

Follow the basics of interviewing when you interview at a temp agency, dress professionally. I know a lot of us don' t like to do this but its something that we have to do. For men if you' re looking for office or sales work put on a nice shirt and slacks and tie or suit and tie. If you' re applying for a labor or warehouse job put on a nice shirt say a polo shirt and slacks not jeans. Now, I know a lot of men hate wearing ties (me included) however it makes you look professional even if the people you' re interviewing with don' t. Comb your hair and make sure you look presentable and professional, a great tip is to stop at the men' s room before interviewing and take a quick look in the mirror. Men when you' re interviewing bring a comb and use it.

Related to dress is your grooming men should make they' re well groomed and their hair looks nice. If you' re in the job market guys its probably a good idea to trim your beard or mustache or shave it off and get a nice short haircut. The more professional you look the better. Its also a pretty good idea to cover up any tattoos that you have.

For the ladies I' d recommend a conservative pants suit or dress and blouse. Don' t put on too much make up or too much jewelry. Make sure the skirt goes below the knees and you don' t show any cleavage. You' re trying to look professional so look professional. If you do wear a skirt it might be a good idea to wear panty hose as well.

One great tip about interviewing for both men and women. Try to dress a cut above the people at the place where you' re interviewing. That will make you look more professional and impressive.

Always try to be on time for an interview at a temporary agency. This means that you should time your journey to arrive at least fifteen minutes early. Arriving early makes you look good and gives you time to take care of paperwork before the interview itself.

The best way to arrive early is make sure you know where you're going. If you have the time do it do a test run a day or so before the interview. Go over there and locate the place and see how long it takes to get there from your home a day or so before the interview. This way you won't get lost and you'll know how long it takes to get there. You can also tell if the directions the temporary agency employees gave you to their office are accurate or not.

One way to help you find your way is to use Google Maps, Yahoo Maps or Mapqwest to create a map to the address. Simply enter the address and these services will tell you where the address is and show you a map. They will also give you directions, personally I prefer maps to directions because I can actually see where I'm going and how to get there. Google Maps is a particularly valuable resource here because it can actually show you a picture of the building and what it looks like from street level.

Once there arrive early and be polite. Don't be a pest remember you're a guest at their office so act like a guest. Follow all the directions from the receptionist or other employ and wait your turn. Be prepared to spend some time there because you may have to wait.

What should you expect at the temp agency? Well most temp agency branches consist of a suite of offices usually located in an office building but sometimes in a shopping center. The agency staff usually consists of several recruiters who handle relations with clients and employees. They are the ones who do the interviewing, place workers, handle the paperwork and sell you to the clients. They' re the ones that you usually have contact with. Most temp agencies also have a secretary or office manager who does the clerical work, answers the phone and greets clients at the door. The office manager is usually the person who gives you your check and handles questions about your pay. Most temporary agencies are quite informal with workers sharing duties and covering for each other. Some temporary agencies also have a concierge who handles relations with employees and provides a variety of services.

When you finally do get called into interview follow the basics of interviewing. Answer all of the questions honestly and make small talk and eye contact. Be as friendly and as personable as possible but watch what you say. Don' t bring up politics, religion or any other potentially controversial topic of conversation. Don' t bad mouth anything or anybody and don' t make any sort of cynical comment or joke. Try to make the best impression that you can.

Listen carefully to what the interviewer has to say and pay attention. One great tip is to ask the interviewer for some input about you they' re a professional and a great resource. Don' t get nervous and if you do have any sort of question ask it. The temporary agency is there to help you find work. Ask the temporary agency employee if there is anything you can do to improve your interviewing and if possible try and schedule a test interview with them.

Ask them about the job market and ask if there are any other jobs for which you might be qualified that are open in your area. They might direct you to some jobs you never thought of and show you how to expand your job search.

One word of advice here if the interviewer asks you to pay any sort of fee and says its required to find work get up and walk out. If they are collecting a fee it is not a real temporary agency it' s a scam designed to get your money. A legitimate temporary agency is paid by the employer when they place you with them. That gives them an incentive to go out and find work for you. An agency that has your money has no incentive to do anything for you after all they have your money.

Another suggestion is to try and avoid interviewing if you feel sick or under the weather. If you get the flu or a cold or a bad allergy attack call the temporary agency and reschedule the interview. When you' re ill you look terrible and you may be too tired to quickly to respond to questions. You may also be irritable and grouchy which won' t make you look good. I might also add that giving a person the flu or a cold is not a good way to make a good impression on them. It' s hard to make a good impression if you' re sneezing or dealing with a runny noise. Rescheduling that interview for a couple of days so you can take it when you ' re on top of your game is probably a good idea.

Always take your time at a temporary agency and be prepared to spend some time there. Some agencies will want to fill out an application and other documents. Some will want you to take tests on computers or watch a safety video. Go along with this because it will help you interview.

Always bring two forms of ID such as your drivers license and social security card to an interview with a temp agency because the temp agency needs a copy of them for federal law. Its also a good idea to bring your check book or a blank check because they may need it to set up direct deposit for your pay. In direct deposit your employer puts your pay directly into your bank account. Direct deposit can save a lot time and hassle. So sign up for it.

A job interview is a two way street a potential employer is using the job interview to evaluate you but a job interview is a great opportunity for you to interview a potential employer. When you interview at a temporary be alert and take a good look around. As you talk to the employees observe how professional they are and ask yourself would you hire a person recommended by these people. If the answer is no then that temporary agency probably won' t do a very good job of finding you work.

Be particularly observant when dealing with the smaller locally run temporary agencies. Some of these mom and pop shops are highly professional but others are strictly amateur hour. Notice if the employees are experienced, articulate and well dressed. Are the offices well kept and well organized? Do they make use of the latest technology? For example: are they professional enough to take job applications online?

If a temporary agency strikes you as amateurish or the recruiters there give you a bad vibe. It would probably be a good idea to look elsewhere. Remember in the average city there are lots of temporary agencies.

Always thank the temporary agency with an e-mail or a phone call after an interview. Try to thank the employ or employees who interviewed you if more than one employee interviewed you thank them all. This shows that you care and more importantly that you' re actively in the job market. It also shows people that you' re a nice person.

### 6.   Make the Temporary Agencies Work for You

Simply registering with a temporary agency is not enough you must learn how to make the temporary agency work for you. This is a lesson that I learned the hard way years ago when I started looking for  work through temp agencies, I registered and then sat around waiting for them to call me with work. Several months passed and I was still sitting around the house next to the phone watching the unpaid bills pile up. That was when I realized that there was more to the process.

Finding work through temporary agencies is an intensive process that involves a lot of input from you. First you must remind the temporary agencies that you' re still alive, that you' re still registered with them and that you' re still looking for work. This means that you have to contact the temporary agencies on a regular basis and tell them these things.

Temporary agency employees are just like other customer service personnel they provide the best customer service to the people who make the most noise. Temp agency workers are most likely to send out resumes from people who make noise, individuals who get their attention and keep it. This doesn' t mean you have to be rude or obnoxious you just have to remind the temp agency that you ' re still in the job market.

The best way to do this is to make a list of temporary agency employees whom you deal with on a regular basis. Then contact them once a week, say on Monday morning and remind them that you' re still in the job market. A great way to do this is by e-mail, simply e-mail the temp agency employees you know every week and tell them that you' re still looking for a job. Or if you prefer the telephone you can call them once a week. This will also show them that you' re conscientious and serious about finding work.

Make a list of the temporary agencies using a program like Microsoft Excel and keep it on your computer. Then once a week or so go through it like a check list and contact all of them. I do it and I' surprised how many calls I' ve gotten back about jobs this way.

Another advantage to e-mailing every week is that you occasionally get that out of the office e-mail telling you to contact somebody else in response. This is a great way to get more contacts at temporary agencies to add to your list.

The more people on your list the more contacts you have for potential job openings.

When you do make contact with these people try and make friends with them. Talk to them about sports or their kids or any other subject that you know they're interested in. See if you share any interests with them and discuss that. A little small talk can transform you into a friend. People are more likely to do a favor for a friend and will be more open with people they like.

When you do talk to the temporary agency employees don't be afraid to pick their minds. Ask them what the job market is like and what jobs are available. Remember they're professionals who know the job market in your area far better than you do. Ask them for advice about interviewing and where to interview. Most importantly ask them if there's anything that you can do to improve your chances of getting hired.

Try and be useful to temporary agency recruiters by doing them some favors or provide them with information. If you know something about jobs or an employer in your area tell the temporary agency professionals that you know about it during your regular contacts. Tell them if you know that a local employer is hiring or if somebody is about to leave their job.

These people make their living by filling empty jobs and they're always on the lookout for new business. If you direct them to some business you'll have done them a favor and they may pay you back by moving your resume to the top of the pile.

Another way to get a temporary agency professional on your side is to be flexible with them. If a temp agency professional calls you about a low paying short term assignment it might be a good idea to take it. If you do them a favor by filling a hard to fill job or going out quickly for work or a job interview you'll have shown them that you're reliable. More importantly you will have done them a favor that they may be obligated to pay you back for. If you do them a favor they may do one for you.

Even going out on a job interview you might not normally go to for a temporary agency can earn you a few points. When a temporary agency employee proposes something to you listen carefully.

You should also avoid doing things that make you look bad in the temporary agency's eyes. Not going out on an assignment or sounding lazy or inattentive can hurt your chances of being sent out. Such actions might even put you on a blacklist which will keep you from working through that agency.

Remember that honesty is the best policy if an assignment sounds like something you really don't want to do, the pay is too low or the job site is too far away for you to commute too tell the temporary agency so. Come out and say that you can't or won't take the job and tell them why.

This will make you look good because you'll appear honest and straight forward. The temporary agency will know that they can trust you and believe what you say. At the same time remember that dishonesty will hurt you if you make a promise you can't deliver on the temporary agency will know that they can't trust you and won't send you out.

You should be honest with the temporary agencies particularly with your resume and job history. You should also be honest about your salary, tell them the minimum wage or salary that you'll work for. That way the temp agency won't be wasting its time calling you with jobs you won't take for financial reasons.

Even when you're registered with temporary agencies you should pay close attention to your local job market. Check the major internet job boards; www.monster.com, www.carreerbuilder.com and www.hotjobs.com on a regular basis say everyday. When you search these boards search by location and date, don' t search just by your specialty because they will give you jobs several months old. One way to save time and effort is to sign up for these boards' e-mail alerts they' ll send you a list of job openings in your field everyday or week. You can easily program monster to search its listings for jobs in your specialty in your area posted in the last few days.

If you see that a temporary agency that you' re registered is advertising a job for which you' re qualified apply for that job. Go to the temporary agency' s website and apply for that job. Then e-mail or phone your contact at the temporary agency and tell them that you' re willing to take that job. Remember temporary agencies have lots of open jobs, and lots of candidates so its easy for them to loose track of you. They may not associate you with a job so remind them that you' re qualified and can take that job.

In addition to the major internet jobs you should check the job postings on the websites of the temporary agencies that you' re registered with at least once a week or more often. The big national temporary agencies post all of their job openings online and update them on a regular basis. Always check these postings, many times I' ve checked them and found jobs posted that I' m qualified for but they never contacted me about. The best way to search most temporary agencies' websites for jobs in your area is to do a geography based searched. You can get a list of jobs in your area by typing in your zip code or your city' s name. Don' t search by specialty just by zip code then look at the list most of the jobs listings will have the dates listed so you can apply to recent jobs in your area.

When you see a job you' re interested in apply for it and more importantly look for the contact information for the person who' s trying to fill that job. Then try and contact them directly and tell them that you' re qualified for that job, willing to fill it and available. Always remind them that you' re already registered with the agency.

You' ll want to contact temporary agencies about job openings they post because turnover at temporary agencies can be high. The person you interviewed with might have left and somebody who doesn' t know you might have taken their place.

Another reason why you' ll need to contact temporary agencies about job postings is that the job may not be posted by the office of the temporary agency you' re dealing with. It might be posted by the national or head office, another office in your area or an office in another city that handles a particular account. The temporary agency employees trying to fill that position might not know about you or your qualifications so introduce yourself by applying.

Always say that you're registered with that agency because dealing with a registered person means less work for temporary agency employees. Temporary agencies look better when they submit a lot of candidates for a job. If you are registered with that agency they can present you as a candidate for a job without doing a lot of work they will be more likely to submit you for work. If you make their job easier, they'll be more likely to help you find a job.

One final suggestion here, its not a bad idea to go in for another interview at the temp agency if you haven't been there in awhile or if the employees ask you to come in. Even if you just drop in and say hi. Actually seeing you reminds them that you're a living breathing human being and a person that they like. It'll give them a little more incentive to find you work.

It's also a good idea to tell a new temporary employee who is unfamiliar with you that you're willing to come in and do another interview or just meet with them. That way you're no longer an unknown quantity to them, you're a person whose strengths and character they're familiar with. If you're nothing but a name on a piece of paper you' ll have a much harder time finding work. Another good thing about interviewing regularly is that keeps you on your toes and prepares you for additional job interviews.

Temporary agencies are a great resource that can help you find work if you' re willing to work with them. More importantly temporary agencies are a resource that will help you find work if you can make them work for you.

### 7.    On the Job

When a temporary agency places you in a position they' ll probably tell you about it via a phone call. Someone from the agency will call you and tell you that you ' ve gotten the job.

Sometimes they' ll tell you to simply report to the jobsite at a certain time to go to work. This is often the case with labor jobs, hospitality jobs and some basic clerical work. The temporary agency employee will call you, tell you where to go, who to report to, what to expect and how to dress for the job.

In these cases you might simply go to the jobsite and report to a particular individual. If a large number of temporary workers are present, somebody from the temporary agency might also be there to brief you and talk to you about the position. Usually you' ll simply report to

43

an individual. Sometimes they' ll put you to work but other times they will assign you to do some training or briefing.

Remember when you' re on the job the person that you' re reporting to is your boss even though the temporary agency is paying you. You' ll have to follow their orders and treat them like your boss. Follow the basics of being a good employee, be conscientious, hardworking, respectful and responsible. Act like you' re a full time employee and put in a full days work. Arrive on time and stay there the entire day.

One word of advice here make sure that you know how to get to the job site before the job. That way you can get there on time and you won' t embarrass yourself and the temp agency by being late.

You should always remember that the person you ' re reporting to will report back to the temporary agency. If they' re impressed with you or like you they' ll say good things about you to the temp agency. If they' re disappointed or disgusted with you they' ll tell the temp agency bad things about you. If the temp agency gets a negative report about you from the client they probably won ' t send you out again.

The major difference between temporary work and regular work will probably be that you will have to fill out a different kind of time sheet or time card. The temporary agency might give you a timesheet that you take to the jobsite. You will have to fill out the time sheet and get the supervisor to sign it. Then you' ll probably have to fax the sheet to the temporary agency. Many of the larger temporary agencies will have you go on line and fill out an online time sheet This is usually easier and more convenient.

Always try and be as impressive as you can on some of the lesser temporary jobs. If you really impress the temporary agency they may send you out on better and higher paying jobs or place you on a long term assignment. A temporary assignment is your chance to try out for a job and to impress potential employers.

Temporary agencies place individuals on several kinds of assignments, there are short term assignments these can last anywhere from a few hours to a few months. Often times people are hired for these assignments because workers are needed for a short period of time or to fill in for somebody who is out.

Many professional assignments are filled on a slightly longer term basis. These can last for a few weeks or a few months. The temporary agency will tell you how long the assignment is and how long can you can expect to be working. The assignment may extended if you do a good job or more work is available. At the same time the assignment maybe suddenly terminated if you're re no longer needed or the client decides they don't t want you for some reason.

You may also hear the term, temp to hire, temp to hire means just that. A person is hired as a temporary worker for a weeks or months and if the employer likes the person they are offered a full time job. A temp to hire position is a try out, the employer gets to see if a potential employee is a good fit for the job and the employee gets to see if they would like working there. Many employers go the temp to hire work because its cheaper and easier than going through a formal hiring process. They get to know the person before they extend a job offer.

Not all long term or professional temporary assignments are temp to hire or will lead to permanent employment. Many large companies now hire a large percentage of temporaries so they can cut staff quickly and not get burdened with lots of employees they'll have to provide benefits for if they are laid off.

One great advantage to such positions is that they give you a chance to broaden your job experience and learn more skills. You can put such longer assignments on your resume and list the experience and skills you honed on those jobs.

### 8.   Interviewing with the Client

Sometimes the temporary agency will ask you to interview with the client before you offering you the position. This interview is just like a regular job interview except you won' t discuss salary or benefits. The temporary agency will tell you what the salary and benefits are before you go out and interview.

Even though this interview has been arranged through a temporary agency you should treat it as a regular job interview. You should dress professionally, arrive on time, and be on your best behavior. You should be respectful and friendly and polite and you should be on your toes. Do your best to try and impress the client because they will be the ones making the decision about whether to hire you or not.

The client will report back to the temporary agency about you. If make a good impression they' ll say good things about you and the temporary agency will arrange more interviews. If you make a bad impression the temporary agency will hear that too and be given a reason not to send you out on more interviews.

One great service that some temporary agencies offer that you should take advantage of is a practice interview. A practice interview is a rehearsal job interview where one of the temp agency employees interviews and evaluates you then shares their results with you.

This service can be really helpful because you can learn what a professional recruiter who interviews a lot of people thinks of you and your interviewing style. They can tell you what you're doing wrong and what you should be doing to get the job. You will learn what you need to do to improve your interviewing and perhaps learn something about yourself. You might even find that you have been sabotaging yourself by doing something wrong in past interviews and not even realized it.

Before you go out to an interview it's a good idea to do a little homework on the company they send you too. One great way to do this is to use the internet, simply go to the client's website. That should tell what you need to know about the company. If you know a little about the company you'll impress the client and can get the job. You should also ask the temporary agency if there's anything that you should be doing.

When you are interviewing be prepared, in particular be ready to answer standard questions asked in interview. Have good answers ready for phrases such as "what is your work style" and "what will you do you do if you miss a deadline." Be honest but try and think these out before the interview so you'll have a good answer ready.

Also be prepared for the unexpected, I've never had an interview where they didn't ask at least unusual or off the wall question that I was totally unprepared for. The way to deal with this is give t he best answer that you can think of. Don't get tongue tied and don't say something stupid. Instead answer honestly and if you don't understand what they're asking ask them what they mean.

Always turn the ringer on your cell phone off when you're at a job interview!! Always!! No phone call is too important to interrupt you when you're interviewing so leave the phone on vibrate. That way you'll know you got the call and you can respond after the meeting. If the phone call is important the person will leave you a message on your voice mail. The last thing you need at an interview is the distraction of a phone call.

If you interrupt your interview to answer the phone you'll look unprofessional and send the message that you don't care about the job. So turn that ringer off and keep it off until after the interview.

Pay attention to the interviewer and listen carefully. Make sure that the job described by the interviewer matches what the temporary agency told you. Be careful that the temporary agency didn' t oversell you. If they have unrealistic expectations about or the position isn' t what the temporary agency described be leery. In particular be careful that they aren' t trying to place you at a position for which you aren' t qualified or simply can' perform. If you don' t think you can do the work or have the skills the interviewer is looking for come out and say so.

The interview can tell you a lot about the temp agency did they do their homework and find a position for which you are qualified. Or did they send out to interview for a job that you won' t get. If it sounds like the temporary oversold you or lied to the client, it would probably be a good idea not to work for that temp agency in the future.

You should also note and see if the temporary agency told you the truth about the client. Is it a place you would like to work and are the people there, individuals with whom you would like to work. Does the workplace' s description the temp agency gave match what you see with your own eyes. If there' s a major discrepancy you might consider going elsewhere.

One interesting suggestion at an interview is take notes, bring a note book and write down some of the things that they ask. Then review the notebook after the interview to see what you learned about the interview. This will show that you are attentive and interested in the job. You'll also have some notes about the interview that you can review afterwards.

After the interview go over the notes and the interview and how it went. Ask yourself what you did right and what you did wrong. Then ask what you can do to improve about your performance. If you become a really good interviewer you'll have a much easier time getting jobs in the future.

The temporary agency will probably ask for a report about the interview after you've completed it usually through a phone call. Be careful but be honest doing this. If something really bothered you about the interview or something didn't feel right tell the temporary agency. Always ask if you're the only person being interviewed and note if they are interviewing people from other agencies.

Mention this fact to your contacts at the temporary agency, because you will be doing them a favor. Many companies will contact several temporary agencies at once about a job and interview candidates from all of those agencies. Interestingly enough they rarely tell the temporary agencies that they' re using the competition. Temporary agency employees like getting this kind of inside information because it helps them get business. Temporary agency employees will pay more attention to people who do them favors.

### 9.  Your Rights as a Temp

As a temp you have the same rights as other workers under the law. The difference is that the temporary agency and not the client is considered your legal employer. Therefore the temporary agency is legally obligated to pay you, provide you with legally mandated benefits,  and pay your withholding, social security, Medicare and other taxes. The temporary agency is also legally responsible if you don ' t get paid, and get hurt or suffer some sort of unsafe or illegal conditions on the job.

The most important legal issue for most workers is getting paid, the temporary agency is legally obligated to pay you all of the money you earned while working for them at the rate they agreed to. Most temporary agencies pay once a week in the form of a direct deposit to your bank account. If you don' t want direct deposit most temporary agencies will cut you a paper check that is sent to your address or picked up by you at the temporary agency. Many temporary agencies have the check in the office for a day or so to let you to pick it up then they mail it to you.

Quite a few temporary agencies including Kelly and Talent Tree are issuing payment cards. These are debit cards in attached to a bank account in which your salary is electronically deposited. You then use the debit card like a credit card to make purchases or get cash through an ATM using a PIN. If you don't want the card you have the option to have the money direct deposited into your checking account. A drawback to the card is that if you want cash you have pay those ATM fees. If you get money out and buy money orders to pay your bills this could get quite costly.

Unfortunately some temporary agencies including Talent Tree have eliminated paper checks entirely. This is probably legal because you sign a contract when you go to work for Talent Tree. So what do you do if you don't have a bank account for direct deposit but you work for an outfit like Talent Tree? This can be a real problem if you can't get a bank account because of a bad credit rating.

There are a now of banks out there that don't run credit checks when you open a checking account. Two of the biggest are Academy Bank which has branches in Wal-

Mart stores in some states and TCF Bank which operates in several states. Another option is an online bank like Account Now. Account Now gives you a debit card and the ability to pay bills using paper checks. You can direct deposit your money into it like any other bank account.

One big advantage employers get from a temp agency is that they can call the temp agency and simply state that they don't want you to come in any more. This makes it real easy to fire or lay off workers. Since the temporary agency is legally your "employer" you're not being laid off.

It's bad because you can get a call right after work saying they don't want you to come in tomorrow morning. There's not much you can do about that but it won't affect your prospects of future employment because the temporary agency won't give you a bad reference. They want you available to go out and get work because that's how they make their money.

This is good because you can quit anytime you want by simply telling the temporary agency that you don't want to come in. That means is if you really don't like the job or get treated badly there or see unsafe conditions you can quit quickly.

You are not legally obligated to stay on a temporary job if there are unsafe working conditions, or you are facing harassment or physical violence. If you face such conditions get up and leave then call the temporary agency and tell them what happened and why you won't go back to that worksite. The temporary agency is still legally obligated to pay you for the hours you worked.

One big question a lot of you are probably asking is what happens if the temporary agency doesn't pay me? Well that probably won't come up I've been working as a temp off and on for over five years and guess what it hasn't happened. Most temporary agencies pay and pay quickly.

The most trouble I had getting a pay check was at a temporary agency that sent my check to a job site several miles away from their office. The assignment had ended so I went over to the office, which was close to my house, to pick up the check and it wasn't there it was at the job site several miles away. Other employees were at the office getting their checks. I raised a fuss and after a short wait the temporary agency cut me a check and handed it to me. I never worked for that agency again but I got my check.

The moral of the story is that if you don't get paid first go to the temporary agency office and tell them so.

Keep records of all the hours you work and compare them to your pay stubs. If you don' t think you' re getting paid then go to the temporary agency and tell them. Do the same if you don' t receive your check or direct deposit. Call and e-mail and if that doesn' t work go and complain.

If your complaints don' t work you can report the temporary agency to your state department of employment. The  temporary agency will get in serious legal trouble if they don' t pay. Tell the temporary agency that you' re going to make such a complaint to give them an incentive to pay you.

You can also take the temporary agency to small claims court if you have legal documentation or if you can locate a group of employees who aren' t paid you could always locate an employment lawyer and file a class action lawsuit against the agency.

Working for a temp agency shouldn' t affect your taxes, they should withhold your federal income tax and your Social Security and Medicare from your pay. Like any other employer a temporary agency should send you a W-2 in the mail or by e-mail in January or February. Just add it when you do your taxes or show it to your taxes like any other employer. If you work for several temporary agencies during the year delay doing your taxes for a couple of months so that you can make sure that you've gotten all of your W-2 forms. Also make sure that you that every temp agency you worked for even ones you aren't working for anymore has your address so they can send you your W-2.

If you don't get a W-2 from a temporary agency call them and ask for it. If they fail to send you a W-2 or claim you didn't work for them. Report that temporary agency to the IRS they are required to send you a W-2 by law. Contact the IRS through its website www.irs.gov. If there's state income tax in your state that will be on the W-2 the temporary agency sends you. The same goes for local income taxes charged by cities and other municipalities.

If you are hurt on the job while working as a temp you are entitled to workman's comp just like any other worker. Contact your state to see what your rights are and how to get workman's comp. If you can't get workman's compensation you might consider finding an employment lawyer. You are also entitled to unemployment insurance if you've done temporary work. You can find out about this by contacting your state government if you live in the USA.

If you think an injury that cost you time on the job was the result of unsafe conditions that the temporary agency or its client were aware of. You may have grounds for a lawsuit, if that's the case contact an employment law or personal injury attorney. You can locate a reputable lawyer through your local bar association. You probably won't to pay the attorney because personal injury attorneys make their money from contingency fees that is they get a piece of any lawsuit or settlement you might get. Most of these lawyers have free consultations. Try and avoid attorneys that advertise on TV and billboards because most of them are shysters.

When you do get hurt on the job many temporary agencies require you to go to their clinic or doctor in order to be covered by their insurance. I don't know if this is legal or not it maybe because you signed a contract for it. This is a situation where you will need to consultant an attorney. Fortunately attorneys who specialize in this area of the law usually have free initial consultations. One simple rule of thumb, if the temporary agency or its attorney tells you don't need a lawyer, that's the minute you need to go out and get a lawyer of your own.

Some temporary agencies do keep a blacklist of employees about whom they have received complaints about from clients. I've been a victim of this practice but it isn't that bad. If a temporary agency blacklists you and says you have a complaint in your file just remember that there plenty of other temporary agencies in the phone book. Simply call one of those and remind the temporary agency that you will be taking your business elsewhere.

I' ve had temporary agency employees tell me that they had received a complaint about me from a client. Then had the same agency call me within the week to offer me another job. Remember temporary agencies make their money by placing people on the job its not in their interests to make people unemployable. In several years of working for temporary agencies I' ve only been blacklisted once by one agency. I had no problem finding work through other agencies.

### 10. Temporary Agency "Benefits"

I' ve noticed that some temporary agencies are offering benefits such as health insurance to temps. My advice to you would be to not use these "benefits" because they don' t appear to be a very good deal.

The health insurance being offered by a number of temporary agencies in Colorado appears to be junk health insurance. That is a policy that will only pay a few hundred dollars which won' t cover the costs of most healthcare. It ' s simply not worth the money the temp agency is taking out of your paycheck.

The best option for people who don't qualify for government health insurance programs like Medicare or Medicaid or state programs would be to see if you qualify for a spouse's health insurance. If your spouse can include you on their insurance you will receive health insurance coverage. So if your spouse gets health insurance through an employer ask if you and your kids can be placed on that policy.

A better solution would be to get your own health insurance through a reputable insurance agency or on line. If you're young and in relatively good health you can probably find a decent policy at a pretty good price. Older people maybe out of luck or they can apply for government programs. There maybe state programs available that you can take advantage of a licensed insurance agent could tell you about them.

A variety of health insurance is available online but choices vary from state to state. People who live in states like Colorado have a lot of choices but individuals in some states such as Alabama have limited choices.

One thing to remember is that health insurance will soon undergo dramatic changes thanks to Congress and President Obama. I don't know what these choices will be but some sort of affordable public or private insurance option may soon be available courtesy of your Uncle Sam.

There are some other good benefits offered by temporary agencies such as training courses for computer software and other topics. If you' re working with a big temp agency you can find out about these through their websites. Some of these courses are a real bargain but they ' re no substitute for college or trade school courses.

### 11. Conclusion and the Future

Temporary agencies will increasingly be the future of work in the United States, millions of us will work for them in the years ahead. This means we should all be familiar with temporary agencies and how they operate.

I have noticed a few trends in the temporary business that could be industry wide changes. The first is virtual and long-distance temp agencies; that is temp agencies or temp agency offices in cities that could be hundreds of miles away placing employees in your area. This will continue as temp agencies try to cut costs.

I live in Denver but in the past few months I' ve dealt with temp agency recruiters in Dallas, Colorado Springs, Rochester, New York and Minneapolis. Interestingly enough I' ve been placed on jobs by temp agency employees in other cities even though those agencies have local offices. Another trend I've noticed is that all the work including the placement will be done by the temporary agency's head office in another city.

The only difference I've noticed from this method is that the contact with the temp agency is through phone, e-mail, fax and mail. Since this is the way you normally contact your temp agency's local office I didn't see much difference. The affect on temporary employees by these changes should be minimal.

One possible development that we will see will be virtual temp agencies which may have no offices. The temporary recruiter works from home, does all the work there and maintains all contact with the temporary employees through e-mail and phone. This will appear because it will cost a lot less than normal temporary agencies because they won't have to rent an office. Under such a system an individual recruiter working from home or a network of such individuals could effectively compete with big national temporary agencies.

A hybrid that I've seen is that the temporary agency employees do most of their work from home but maintain an office for interviews. The office may have a secretary or clerk who maintains contact with employees who walk in.

These changes shouldn' t have much impact on temporary workers but they will make temporary work cheaper and more widespread. Increasing the number of temporary agencies should increase the number of opportunities available to workers. Unfortunately these changes will make it easier to set up fly by night agencies that rip off unsuspecting job seekers and employers so be leery.

Temporary agencies have a very bright future and are now the best job hunting resource available to Americans. Everybody who' s looking for work should take advantage of them.

## A Short List of Temporary Agencies

**Accountemps**
www.accountemps.com
**Adecco**
www.addeco.com
**Aerotek**
www.areotek.com
**Ajillon**
www.ajillon.com
**Appleone**
www.appleone.com
**Express Personnel**
www.expresspersonnel.com
**Kelly Services Inc.**            www.mykelly.com
**Manpower Inc.**
www.manpower.com
**Office Team**            www.officeteam.com
**Randstaad**            www.randstaad.com
**Robert Half Inc.**
www.roberthalf.com

Please Note that there are many more temporary agencies most of which can easily be located on line. Simply type the words temporary agencies and the name of your city into your search engine and it should give you a list.